AF428026

Paperback: ISBN 979-8-9889822-1-0
First Paperback Edition: September 2023

Written by: Mina Soliman
Illustrated by: Cynthia Zeilenga

BCZ Publishers
3365 E Miraloma Ave Ste 205, Anaheim, CA 92806

how i helped...
Daniel in the Lion's Den

"Be strong and courageous. Do not be afraid or terrified because of them, for the Lord your God goes with you; he will never leave you."
Deuteronomy 31:6

Somewhere out in the wild
In a field of trees and dandelions
There lived beasts of all shapes and sizes
Including my pride of hungry lions

I was proudly meaner than the rest
Wanting nothing but to hunt and eat
So vicious, like I was possessed
Always roaming the land on my feet

6

One day, as I was wandering around
I heard a loud sound banging
There I saw a huge box on the ground
Inside, was a piece of juicy meat hanging

I sprang towards the box and jumped right in
Without even a thought of looking around
I grabbed the meat viciously with my mouth
But as I turned to leave, the box came crashing down

10

Several men joyously jumped out of the brush
And quickly carried the box and me in chains
They sold me to a kingdom of royals
Ensuring I would never again roam the wild plains

In the kingdom where I was taken
Lived a faithful man named Daniel
He loved God with all his heart
And served King Darius without a single scandal

While the rest of the kingdom lived in its wealth and riches
Daniel lived true to God wholehearted
Earning favor from King Darius for reading his visions
While his other servants jealously plotted

17

These men conspired against Daniel
And tried to turn the King's favor
But try as they could to make Daniel fall
One thing was sure, his faith in the Lord would never waiver

In the midst of the turmoil, I arrived at the palace
And all of the men feared as I paced around
The cage lowered and the door was opened
Where I walked into a den underground

Envy had taken over the kingdom
They tricked King Darius to place a rule on all men
Resulting in Daniel being sentenced unfairly
And thrown into the lions' den

24

The other lions and I were starving
When suddenly the cave door rolled open
The man they called Daniel was thrown in
But he had no fear and a spirit unbroken

25

As we all eagerly circled around him
An angel suddenly appeared with a stretched out arm:
"This is a man of God," the angel pronounced
"To him shall come no harm"

I immediately felt the peace of this man
And even reflected on my past days
Living for nothing but to take and consume
I knew I needed to change my future ways

King Darius opened the lions' den
And rejoiced greatly when he found Daniel safe and sound
He praised God for this great miracle
And in turn threw the evil men on the lions' ground

That day the whole kingdom and I learned God's lesson
With eyes and spirit open, we could finally see
How God works in mysterious ways
Using the traps of greed and envy, to set us all free

33

The End.